T0161048

Catherine's Laughter

CATHERINE'S LAUGHTER

C. K. Williams

Quarternote Chapbook Series #11

Sarabande  Books

LOUISVILLE, KENTUCKY

Managing Editor
Sarabande Books, Inc.
2234 Dundee Road, Suite 200
Louisville, KY 40205

Library of Congress Cataloging-in-Publication Data

Williams, C. K. (Charles Kenneth), 1936–
  [Poems. Selections]
  Catherine's laughter / C.K. Williams. — First Edition.
      pages cm. — (Quarternote Chapbook Series ; #11)
  ISBN 978-1-936747-68-9 (paperback : acid-free paper)
  I. Title.
  PS3573.I4483C38 2013
  813'.54—dc23
                                    2013011787

Cover and text design by Kirkby Gann Tittle.

Manufactured in Canada.

This book is printed on acid-free paper.

Sarabande Books is a nonprofit literary organization.

The Kentucky Arts Council, the state arts agency, supports Sarabande Books with state tax dollars and federal funding from the National Endowment for the Arts.

Catherine's Laughter

CATHERINE

"How do you say it? Cat-ah-reen?"
"No, Cat-reen. And roll the "r" a little."
"Cat-ghreen?"
"Almost."

CHARLES

For quite awhile after Catherine and I met, the occasion never arose for her to call me by my name, I was just "you," or "tu," or "mon amour." The first time I heard her refer to me, talking to one of her sisters, by my name, "Charles", with the French pronunciation—"Shaarl," it rhymes with "gnarl"—I was taken aback, and she admitted she had been a little, too.

We laughed about it, but even so, when she addresses me by my name now instead of "Tu," the reason has to be examined: she's irritated or exasperated with me, the distance between my tidy, compact pronoun and my gnarly proper noun pounds like a surf, and I begin to understand those cultures where everyone keeps their true name to themselves. What you let out—Charles, for me—isn't really who you are.

I forget whether in those places you ever reveal your real name, even to your loved ones, lest they betray it, but how could they do that?

HER LAUGHTER

There's no reserve, no hanging back in it, no thought of decorum, no thought of anything apparently except whatever has amused her or given her delight. It can also be splendidly . . . what? Hearty, raucous? No, those words are too coarse: her laughter always has something keen and sweet to it, an edge of something like song. It has volume, too, of course: in a group of people I can always hear her laughter soaring above everyone else's. Once, in a movie theater in New York, watching a French comedy much of the humor of which was lost in the subtitles, she laughed alone for almost the whole film, completely by herself, and never noticed.

When we first were together, I used to try to find a metaphor, a figure to specify what her laughter was like. What came closest was one of those funny, clunky wooden pull-toys kids used to have, might still have for all I know—a duck, a too-long dachshund, a tiny elephant. I remember our son Jed had one, a bee, yellow and black with droll resilient spring-antennas and segmented legs.

Sometimes Jed would tug the bee behind him without bothering to look. The thing might not even be on its wheels anymore, it would just be bouncing helter-skelter, wonkety-wonk along, ricocheting onto its imperturbable nose, wobbling, rolling, bumping, snagging on cracks in the sidewalk, making brave little leaps like a salmon.

Like that her laughter was, and is, when something strikes her as funny, and she's already happy, which she almost always is—just like that, a toy a child is dragging unselfconsciously behind, just like that.

SQUELCHED

Sometimes her laugh gets squelched somewhere under her throat; it's trying to rise but she's holding it back, keeping it in its little cage.

This is when she's said something she knows is funny, and you're laughing. She tries to hold her face still, but her smile is so eager to insinuate itself into her voice she can hardly manage it, her eyes close with it, her torso struggles not to quake, rock with it, her lips are screwed shut, then she can't do it anymore, the laughter erupts, the notes of it shine through, it's here, it's arrived.

"What a pleasure," a friend once remarked, "to make that woman laugh."

FUNNY

Jessie, my daughter, when she was eight, already the warm and loving person she still is, said to me once when Catherine was laughing about something with Jed in the other room, "Catherine laughs funny, doesn't she?"

"It's nice, though, isn't it?" I asked her.

"Oh, yes, that's not what I mean," she replied.

And Jed, when he was three, and still spoke mostly French, would sometimes be uproariously amused by an English word. "Inch," when I said it to him one day, sent him into hysterics.

Catherine was in the kitchen right then and when I went in to get something, she said, "Jed has a funny laugh, don't you think?"

"What do you mean?" I asked her, "he has your laugh."

"Really?" Catherine said. "Well, if you say so."

NOT

However reckless and abandoned and contagious and unabashed her laughter might be, even when she's wholly taken by something, it's never too much. Not too much, the way, once, at a party we gave, to which a friend brought both his wife and mistress who'd supposedly achieved a truce of some sort, the lover laughed.

The wife, that evening at least, was buying none of their ostensible truce, she occupied herself entirely and quite openly contemptuously with the other wives and girl-friends, while the mistress, (she'd soon leave our friend, devastating him) sat with the men, the husbands and boy-friends, gabbing with them, laughing, shooting the shit. . . .

Not that laughter, not ever for a moment that husband-laughter, lover-laughter, that stoical laughter that slapped its knee, elbowed your ribs, told dirty jokes. . . .

I've never heard that laughter from Catherine, I hope I never have to.

REAL BEES

Jed, three or four then, and Catherine and I are watching a nature program on television about the life of insects, photographed by one of those new micro-cameras—life in a hive, in a drop of water, that sort of thing. It turns out to be very funny, a trap-door spider popping up like a jack-in-the-box to grab a passing beetle, an ant ponderously hauling a mighty crumb.

We're all laughing together, but Catherine's transported. A scene with flying bees bumping into one another and falling all over themselves like incompetent little airplanes she finds hilarious, she's absolutely rhapsodic about it, each moment of the film is funnier to her than the last, her laughter fills the room, and at one point Jed and I both look away from the screen and glance at her, then we look at each other, our gazes meet briefly—Catherine still in the midst of one of her peals of delight—and something passes between us: we're caught together in some unspoken, never to be spoken of conspiracy, beyond us both.

CRAZY

Maybe it's just my age, but sometimes these days when I'm making love to Catherine it feels as though I'm really making love as much, or more—no, that's going too far, just as much—to her beauty. Is this unusual? Unhealthy? I have no idea. When I tell Catherine, she says she never thinks of herself as beautiful.

That's crazy, I say, you're fibbing.

No, she insists. . . . Then, she admits, maybe once. When she was sixteen or so, in a resort town somewhere with her parents, she noticed people looking at her differently from the way they always had. She went back to her room and looked into the mirror, and she did indeed look beautiful to herself.

That's the only time, though.

Ha, I say: What about when O—— tried to kiss you? What about when M—— tried to hold your hand?

She laughs, "Okay, maybe once or twice."

Ha. Once or twice. Ha.

HER BEAUTY

Men often find Catherine beautiful, and besides that the kind of beauty she has seems to make them feel free to tell her. "Beautiful," said a normally quite reserved, not to say quite often irascible sociologist friend when he met Catherine on the first walk she and I took when we came from Paris to Philadelphia. I introduced Catherine, he looked at her, shook her hand and said it: "Beautiful." Just like that, not "She's beautiful," not, "You're beautiful," just, "Beautiful."

Which might seem odd, except it's precisely what a very unreserved poet, well known for his exuberance, said, too, also shaking her hand, when he met Catherine at one of his readings: "Beautiful."

Some other friends, too, a painter, another poet, same thing: "Beautiful," just like that, just that.

And I guess I should mention the famous man I won't name here who didn't say "beautiful" when Catherine and I met him at a conference, but who, I found out from her after he died, had tried, unsuccessfully thank goodness, to convince her to come to his hotel room. I, vigilant as I am—I really am, because I'm so fearfully jealous—suspected nothing, which I'm glad about now because we came to cherish the man later as a friend, and it would have been difficult for me if I'd known.

The strangest thing is when I first met Catherine, I didn't think of her as all that beautiful. Nice looking, certainly, pretty; but not really beautiful. I've often wondered why, but I can't remember and I can't remember either when I did start thinking of her as beautiful. When we first met—it was at Kennedy airport, our plane to Paris was ridiculously late—she was standing patiently in the line of passengers, and smiled in commiseration at me, I suppose already recognizing my pain-in-the-neck impatience. She was dressed, I remember perfectly, in a shleppy, shapeless black sweater, not very flattering jeans, and wore big eyeglasses. I smiled back but moved away because I was trying to find out what the hell was going on and the airline people were being very unhelpful.

After a few hours we were told the plane still hadn't arrived from Europe but that we'd be taken out to dinner. A bus came, I got on and Catherine sat beside me. We didn't get to Paris for another day and a half, and by then we were friends, and soon after and ever since lovers.

Back to her beauty. I've been in quite a few situations when someone we don't know will look across a dinner table, say, and I'll realize that Catherine's beauty has suddenly dawned on them. There's always a slight look of surprise in their expression, almost shock, as though a light had been turned on around Catherine. And that's just what it's like: when Catherine becomes interested in something, animated, involved in a conversation, an idea, an emotion, she takes on a kind of glow. I really can't explain it: she's just all at once beautiful, to me more beautiful.

I enjoy when that happens, when people—I purposefully don't say "men" because it happens with women, too—will fall in something like love with her. Sometimes, if the person is an attractive male, it doesn't make me terrifically happy. As I say, I'm painfully jealous, but I survive.

JEWELS

Catherine and I, a few days after we met, are taking a walk on one of the fanciest upscale streets in Paris. We pass by the most elegant of all the jewelry stores—money all but drips from the facade.

"I once had a bracelet from there," Catherine remarks.

"Where is it now?" I ask her.

"I sold it to pay for my divorce."

"Who gave it to you," I ask, "your ex-husband?"

"No."

"Who then?"

"An admirer."

"An *admirer?*"

She'd never tell me who.

JEALOUSY

I try, without immediately laughing aloud, to consider seriously the proposition that Catherine might be jealous of *me*. I make a little psychic drama in which I'm in conversation with someone, anyone, it doesn't matter, and that she's looking across at me and smoldering, quavering, dissolving with anxiety and fret.

Utterly impossible. She couldn't know, couldn't suspect, couldn't have the wildest imagination of what it would be like.

Here's what it's like: I'm watching her, at a party, say, a restaurant, a gallery, conversing with another man, someone she evidently admires, perhaps feels affection for, perhaps, I think, incipient love for, sexual passion for. Of course I keep my mouth clamped, sealed, hammered, nailed, screwed shut.

When I consider what to do next, the only solution I can posit is to become inanimate, and the shortest route to that would be to become one with the chair in which I sit. My all at once beloved chair: its back is almost precisely the length of my spine, and its seat—think!—has more legs than I have! What relief! I am the chair that holds me, that holds me up. I am chair.

But now an army of ravenous invisible birds approaches the foot of the cherished chair to harvest the crumbs of my psyche as it disintegrates and dissolves. Secret birds: their eyes shine like the nails of a nurse preparing for your operation.

Then the crumbs are gone, devoured, there's nothing left of me, psyche, body, brain, and so the birds, in a disanesthetizing gleaming shudder and fly away.

It goes on . . . I wait, I watch, I count, my heartbeats, my brain waves, but the chair is growing tired, it bends one leg, then another. My chair, poor chair, it doesn't even have eyelids to swing down like shutters. . . . Or do I mean shudders?

What do I mean? I forget what I might mean, or anything might mean. I find I envy now the placid, stupid four-square tables, then the lamps that perch on them and burn, burn if they desire all the endless night.

Like them, I burn, I watch, with something like a mighty winch I haul my eyes agape and watch.

FASTER

When the workmen came to unclog the cess-pool of the tiny house in Greece Catherine and I had rented those first weeks we were together, they heaved the syrupy shit-gunk into the shallow cove in front of our terrace, and it settled through the vividly clear water into a grey layer on the rocks and pebbles at the bottom and stayed there.

The reason they did it was because the water that fed the house had been contaminated, but it was even more foul now—we couldn't drink it, cook or even shower with it. There was a well, though, a little way up the hill behind us, and we'd walk there with a big ceramic jug to rinse ourselves off. The water was clean, but icy cold— I hated it.

Catherine appeared not to mind, but when I'd pour the water over her head and it would run down over her body, her skin would erupt in goose-bumps—what a crude term for such a lovely phenomenon—and she'd all at once possess a different sort of corporality, solidity, depth.

"Breathtaking," another absurdly inadequate word, but my breath really would be taken—I'd gasp, my breathing would stop, then start again, faster, faster.

PAINTING

Catherine and I are renovating our new apartment and for the last four days I've been scraping off wallpaper, the worst job on earth, the most repetitive and boring, and all the while Catherine's been busy with other things, taking care of Jed, going to her job at a jewelry workshop, so she hasn't been here at all, it's been just me hour after hour with the miserable steaming machine and the clumsy putty knives. We've agreed I'll take the afternoon off for some work chores I have to finish by tomorrow, and she's already ten minutes late.

Now she's finally here. I hear her key at the door, hear her footsteps in the hallway, hear her come to the room, and there she is. She's dressed in old sneakers, worn jeans and an old down jacket of mine which it goes without saying is much too big for her, so she has the air of a kid dressed up in adult clothes, and also she's carrying a paper bag the contents of which I can't figure out.

"Voilà, here I am," she says, looking around at the scraps of ancient wallpaper and the fragments of old molding on the moldy carpet. I'm impatient for her to get to work, though, and she knows I am—the whole atmosphere of the room is declaring, "Let's get to work." But first . . . out of her mysterious bag she plucks. . . . What? Her radio, for goodness sake, her ridiculous out of date radio, and she holds it up even though we both know the time's past for screwing around and says, "Where's the plug?"

"Where's the damned plug?" is what I want to answer, but when I look at her she looks suddenly like Charlie Chaplin, or maybe Stan Laurel, and she knows it, and knows too that I know it and we both know how silly this is and how sweet—it's a scene from some comic movie, and we both must think that at the same instant so that after a pause just the duration Chaplin would have been pleased with I get off the ladder, embrace her, and we laugh, and kiss, I leave, and yes, she really does get to work so that when I come back a few hours later she's scraped the paper off the whole dining-room ceiling, a task I'd been dreading—it's an offering for me from her, as though I needed another.

ANNIVERSARY

"It's not so bad all the time being married to you," Catherine tells me.

"You mean it's not bad being married to you all the time."

"No, I mean it's not bad all the time being married to you."

LATER

It must have been after some intense discussion, not an argument, nothing personal, just my usual gloom erupting that Catherine wrote in pencil on a sheet of "While You Were Out" paper that I came across in a pile of papers months later, long after I'd forgotten what we might have been disagreeing about: "Differ without rancor as a man may differ with himself. . . ."

I have no idea where she found the quote, but underneath it, in blue ink in my hand is written: "I differ from myself with rancor."

Then in pencil under that, in her writing again, "You're stupid, that's why."

MISCARRIAGE

When we had the miscarriage, that fearsome middle of the night bleeding, frantic calls to the doctor, "Rest. . . . Wait. . . ." then so much blood, gouts splattering the floor, the bed and sheets soaked. . . .

When after the surgery, Catherine came back, she couldn't or wouldn't wake from the anesthesia. The surgeon kept urging her, "Wake up now, open your eyes!" flicking a fingernail on the side of her hand, but her eyes stayed sealed, she seemed to be hardly breathing, and finally the doctor told me to try.

I was frightened—how much she must have wanted to stay where she was, how reluctant to come back—but I tried: "Open your eyes, love. . . . Faut te reveiller. . . ."

Her lips moved a little, her eyelids fluttered almost imperceptibly.

"Okay," the doctor said, "let her sleep now," and she did sleep, for hours and hours while I waited for her to wake again.

DANCE

Catherine studied ballet when she was young; she never talks about it, but once, in the most boring room of a depressing museum in Denmark, she suddenly whirled three perfect piqué turns across the floor and ended up out in the corridor, ready, to my relief, to leave.

PERFUME

Catherine is drying herself off after her bath; she has a tiny vial of perfume and she dabs some on the back of her neck.

"What's that?" I ask her.

"Come here," she says, "they gave it to me in a store, it's for men."

She puts some on my hair.

"Not on my hair," I say, "it stinks."

I take the vial. It's called "Yatagan," or some crap like that. "Look," I say, "even the name is ridiculous."

"Well," Catherine says, "we'll find some perfume for you with a nice virile name."

"Like what?" I ask.

"How about 'Dung?'" she answers.

"Dung?" I say, "*dung?*"

Catherine laughs, "Close the door."

SULKING

We've been spatting and sulking and brooding and sizzling; I go teach my class, come home, Catherine's at her work-bench, and, though it's not easy, "I'm sorry," I say, "I was really depressed, I just wanted some solace."

Catherine's still angry: "Maybe I'm depressed, too," she answers. I'm stunned, then angry again. "What should I say?" I ask her, "that I was first, that I was depressed first?"

Catherine turns her head away from me, then after a moment I notice that her shoulders seem to be shaking a little. For a moment I can't tell for sure what's going on: she's not saying anything but more of her body is shaking, and then it breaks through, her laughter, she's laughing. I'm saved! Free!

I touch her, she leans back against me, laughing; her body against me has such solidity now, I can feel the mus-cles in her shoulders, the flat bones on her back mov-ing under my hands—those "wings," we call them, as we should.

TUESDAYS

When some friends left their two daughters, seven and five, with us to take care of for a few hours, Catherine told them stories, two of her favorite fairy tales. One I hadn't heard before was about a king who falls in love with a beautiful princess who agrees to marry him on one condition: that on Tuesdays she has to be alone—he can't see her or talk to her, she just has to be allowed to stay by herself in her room.

The king agrees, they marry, they're very happy except that the king becomes curious, then obsessed, as we will, by what in heaven's name could be going on on Tuesdays in that room, and one day he breaks open the door to see. When he enters, his wife sadly looks at him, turns into a blackbird and flies out the window.

The king is devastated, needless to say, and in the original, that's the end of the tale—I suppose the moral is don't be so nosy, something like that.

But when Catherine tells me about telling it to the girls, she felt she had to add a different ending: one day the king is moping in tears through his estate and another blackbird approaches him and asks him what's wrong. He confesses the error he'd made and the blackbird tells him he'll have another chance, that he should go home.

He goes back to his palace and there's his wife again waiting for him. He's overcome with joy, and they live happily ever after.

Except of course, Catherine laughs when she tells me, on Tuesdays.

TALK

Catherine and I, for some long forgotten reason, have both been irritable all day, touchy, preoccupied, moody and gloomy. Dinner is peaceful, though, and when we finish Catherine asks, "Are we going to make love tonight?"

I answer, "If I'm talking to you."

"You don't have to talk," Catherine says.

BREEZE WITH FLOWERS

A puff, and the flowers jerk in erratic little spasms, as, when we make love, her body will sometimes move gently to no rhythm. A larger gust then and they spin at the limit of their attachment, until, becalmed, they're released back into their decorous stillness, as when, after, she is often taken by an engrossing, enviable calm.

The breeze again: the flowers all lean in the same direction, like sopranos reaching for a note, (and aren't they, the flowers, voices without singers, exalting with and to one another in their fragrant silence?) as her voice becomes other than voice, more than voice, finds more voices in her voice.

Beneath, the leaves and stems shuffle together, like corps of violinists, dutiful, dedicated, constant, then are still again, as I, dedicated, constant, lie beside her now, constant, stilled.

THE FIRST TIME

The first and I'd wager the only time I'll ever fall asleep laughing Catherine and I had been making love earlier in the evening and lost track, so to speak, of our route, and tipped off the bed onto the floor. Such a tangle of limbs and buttocks bouncing on the hard wood, but Catherine of all things began laughing and kept laughing for a bit even after we were back in bed, but she'd hit her head on the bedside table and when we got up for dinner she had a swelling on her forehead, which she put ice on, and some French homeopathic gunk she believes in.

Then, later, when we went to bed, I reached over I thought very gently to pat her head to see how she felt but just then she moved towards me so that my hand bumped right onto where she was bruised, and, "So," she said, "are you going to attack me again?" and burst out laughing again, and what else could I do but laugh, too, and we both couldn't stop, lying there laughing, laughing together as we held each other and drifted away.

DOGS

When she walks our dog Catherine tends to be a bit oblivious to how much mischief Bwindi might effect. She lets her wander at the end of her leash, even in the middle of town; sometimes the leash will get entangled around people's legs, and once, Bwindi snatched a croissant out of the hand of a baby in a stroller. The baby howled, Catherine was very embarrassed and offered to buy another, but the amused mother declined.

When Catherine tells about that, she laughs, but recently there was a more dramatic incident. She was walking through the town near where we live when we're in France, and a woman, when she saw Bwindi approaching on her loose leash, stopped dead on the sidewalk, obviously frightened. Catherine noticed, brought Bwindi against her legs, and asked the woman what was wrong. The woman responded that she had a terror of dogs: she was Jewish, and when she was four during the war, German soldiers came with police dogs and took away her parents and brother and sister and she never saw them again.

Hardly surprising she wouldn't care for dogs. She and Catherine chatted awhile and the woman told how she'd been saved when she'd been left alone in Paris, that she'd been sent to be brought up by a couple here in this town where she still lived.

Some years ago I saw a show in a museum of photographs of French people who had helped Jews during the Nazi frenzy, taking them into their homes, hiding them, bringing them up as their own children. I wanted to write about it, but nothing I could say came close to doing justice to what was visible in the saved and saviors in those pictures: their simple, factual presences, no glow, no halos, nothing exalted in their expressions: they were real, as we all are, and that was enough.

In this case, though, it didn't turn out so well. The woman had been very unhappy with the couple who'd adopted her, and had had what sounded like a generally unfulfilling life.

Catherine was moved—that's not the way you want stories like that to end. But even the beginning…Catherine was only a few years younger than the woman; they'd both been born in Paris, perhaps blocks from one another. If Catherine had been a Jew. . . .

There are matters that can't be coped with in reflecting on life, or love, or sometimes it seems anything at all.

LOOBAHSH

Catherine reads a lot, and quickly, and often listens to authors on the radio, both in France and in the States, then buys their books. Though very few turn out to be as interesting as their authors have made them sound, this doesn't deter her, she still listens, and buys, and reads.

When she brings a book to bed, as she always does before we go to sleep, she puts her feet up on the wall over the headboard. As she reads, one heel will rub lightly over the shin on her other leg, then go out straight so her legs are parallel again, lines ending in infinity, I think. Then the other leg will bend, move against the first, straighten out again and aim again.

Tonight, earlier in the evening we'd watched a DVD of a Hungarian movie, very stark, gloomy, about starving peasants, a father and daughter, and the peasants' broken-down, ill horse, and also, the last moments of the film implied, though you couldn't be certain, the end of the world. Much darkness, much raw fear.

There was very little dialogue, mostly single word ejaculations the father and daughter passed between them and almost all of which were subtitled as, "Fuck!" Their horse is dying: "Fuck!" Their well has run dry: "Fuck."

Later, Catherine in bed reading, me getting undressed, something falls clattering from her bedside table, Catherine mutters, "Fuck!" and I say, "That's what they said in the movie."

And Catherine, who didn't care for the film and only watched parts of it, says without looking up from her book, "Loobahsh."

"What?" I ask. "Is that the word?"

"Loobahsh," she says again, a grain of laughter in her voice.

"You made that up," I say to her. "Very funny."

Again, with a chuckle, "Loobahsh . . . Loobahsh."

Her left heel runs over her right shin, flexes, straightens, parallel with the other, both legs aiming out once more toward the planets and stars.

OAKS

After dinner, still at the table, I'm writing in my little note-book, scribbling fast, when Catherine says she'd like to take a walk. When I tell her I'm busy she takes the empty dishes into the kitchen, then comes back.

"Come on, take a walk."

"I'm writing," I tell her.

"Take your notebook. You can take your wine, too."

"Wait just a minute," I say.

"You need a bigger notebook," Catherine says then, "I'll buy you a bigger notebook."

"I don't need a bigger notebook, and don't get me one."

"That's why I said it," Catherine says, "I just wanted to hear you say that. Let's go for a walk."

Finally I give up, give in, we stroll out across the park near our house, and come to the pair of gigantic old oaks Catherine particularly loves. The trunk of each tree is about five feet across, and they stand close together, leaning a lit-tle as though making room for one another.

They're in full-leaved gorgeousness right now, and when we get to them Catherine says, "You have to come in here," and leads me between them.

"Now close your eyes," she says.

"Why?"

"Because there are all those branches above us," she answers, "and beneath us the roots. You have to listen."

I listen, "But I don't. . . ." I start to object.

"You have to come stand here every day, then you will," Catherine answers, not laughing now, "You'll see, you will."

C. K. Williams has won the Pulitzer Prize, the National Book Award, the National Book Critics Circle Award, and the Ruth Lilly Prize, among other honors. In 2010 he published the critical study, *On Whitman*, and a book of poetry, *Wait*. In 2012 he published the poetry collection *Writers Writing Dying* and a book of essays, *In Time: Poets, Poems, and the Rest*. He is a member of the American Academy of Arts and Letters.

Sarabande Books thanks you for the purchase of this book; we do hope you enjoy it! Founded in 1994 as an independent, nonprofit, literary press, Sarabande publishes poetry, short fiction, and literary nonfiction—genres increasingly neglected by commercial publishers. We are committed to producing beautiful, lasting editions that honor exceptional writing, and to keeping those books in print. If you're interested in further reading, take a moment to browse our website, www.sarabandebooks. org. There you'll find information about other titles; opportunities to contribute to the Sarabande mission; and an abundance of supporting materials including audio, video, a lively blog, and our Sarabande in Education program.